# Youth SOCCER UNLEASHED

A Parent's and Player's Guide to the Fundamentals of the Game

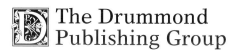

The Drummond
Publishing Group

Printed in the United States

ISBN 0-975-5080-0-8

Library of Congress Control Number: 2004106458

# CONTENTS

**History  1**

**Warm-up and Basic Skills  5**

Warm-Up Exercises  6

Dribbling  8

Trapping  12

Passing  16

Heading  18

Juggling  20

Shooting and Other Kicks  22

Throw-ins  25

Shielding  26

Marking  28

Tackling  30

Goalkeeping  32

**Rules and Regulations  35**

Recommended Field Sizes  37

Recommended Ball Sizes  37

Player Positions  38

Player Equipment  39

Referees  40

Duration of the Game  44

Start of Play  44

The Ball In and Out of Play  45

Scoring  45

Offside  45

Fouls and Misconduct  46

Cautions and Ejections  46

Free Kicks  47

Penalty Kicks  48

Throw-ins  48

Goal Kick  49

Corner Kick  49

**Dictionary of Common Soccer Terms  50**

**Games  57**

# HISTORY

**G**ames like soccer have been played for thousands of years. The Chinese played Tsu-Chu about 3,000 years ago. In Japan, they played Kemari at about the same time. The early Greeks had a game called Episkyros. The Romans brought Harpastum to ancient Britain, and this may be the game that developed into soccer.

In 1904 the Fédération Internationale de Football Association (FIFA) was formed. There are now more than 150 member nations and soccer is played around the world. The World Cup, first held in 1930 and played every four years, is one of the most widely watched sports events in the world.

Soccer is an easy game to learn; the rules are simple. It can be played by both boys and girls, and it is relatively inexpensive. Today, nearly every major city and town in the U.S. has a youth soccer program, and more than 17 million boys and girls in kindergarten through high school participate nationally.

# Youth Soccer in Brief

Soccer is the world's most widely played team game, because it is easy to learn and fun for girls and boys of all ages. The key to soccer is teamwork—each team works as a unit to score goals and defend its own goal.

The team concept starts early, where the youngest play in 3 v. 3 games. Youth soccer groups add more players, as players get older, until they reach 11 v. 11 games. No matter how many people, though, the most successful teams with the happiest players are the ones that work well together.

It may look like some players are on offense and some on defense, depending on where they play on the field. But really, all players help in both areas.

All of your skills are important, but nothing is more important than you and your teammates playing as a team.

Each team must move the ball up the field to score, without touching the ball with arms or hands, and this requires ball control. No matter what your position on the field, soccer requires good footwork, passing, trapping, and kicking, and it requires quick thinking and the ability to take the ball from the other team. The fundamental skills taught in this book are the building blocks for good ball control, offensive and defensive play, and, ultimately, teamwork. Of course, you can never master these skills without practice. The more you touch the ball, the better you become!

The rules in the second half of the book show the particulars—what moves are illegal, what the referee is saying, and what types of penalties are issued for breaking the rules.

More than anything, soccer is about fun. It's great exercise, it builds teamwork, and it can be thrilling for players and parents. The best way to experience it is to play it and play it often. So take a peak at what's inside, get familiar with the essentials, and get a ball and hit the field!

# WARM-UP AND BASIC SKILLS

# Warm-Up Exercises

At the beginning of every practice, you should warm up and stretch your muscles. Start by jogging around the field. Then do as many of these stretches as you have time for before starting practice or playing. Stretch slowly; don't jerk, bounce, pull, or hold a stretch until it hurts. Stretches are to loosen the muscles. If you push too hard, the end result is a tight muscle. A stiff or tight muscle is more likely to be strained.

◀ **Groin stretch:** Use your hands to gently push out and down on your knees. Hold for 5–8 seconds.

▶ **Spine twist:** Cross your left leg over your knee, and bend your right elbow to keep your leg and hips from turning. Put your left arm behind you for support. Turn your head to look over your left shoulder. Hold for 10–15 seconds. Reverse to stretch your right side.

▶ **Calf stretch:** Push forward with your hips. Hold for 15 seconds. Your feet need to be facing straight forward, or with toes slightly inward.

◀ **Back, shoulders and arms:** Bend to one side and hold for 8–10 seconds, then repeat for the other side.

▼ **Groin, hip, and quadriceps:** Push down at your hips. Hold for 15 seconds for each leg.

▶ **Hamstring stretch:** Stretch down from the hips toward your outstretched foot. Hold for 10–15 seconds for each leg.

Warm-Up Exercises

N ow that you know how to warm-up, you're ready for the game's skills. What follows are the keys to good ball control, offense, and defense. You need to understand each move and know how to execute it. The illustrations and explanations will get you started. But the best way to master skills is practice— "touching," or playing with, the ball every day. So get to know the terms and techniques, then get a ball and practice.

## Dribbling

Moving the ball along the ground with your feet is called dribbling. Dribbling is good for keeping control of the ball when you can't safely pass it to a teammate, but you need to keep the ball moving and away from the other team.

▶ Start with the foot closest to the ball. Using either the inside or outside of your foot, touch the ball gently about halfway up the ball to move it in the direction you want to go. Pass the ball from one foot to the other always keeping the ball under control. You should push or sweep the ball along, not kick it.

You can use all parts of the shoe for control while dribbling. Touching the ball with the inside part keeps the ball in front of you. Touching the ball with the outside allows you to change direction and move past defenders. The toe and heel can be used to stop the ball suddenly or change its direction suddenly.

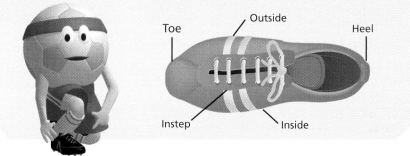

Using the inside of foot ▶

▼ Using the outside of foot

Using the toe ▶

**Remember to keep your head up so you can see where you are going.**

## PRACTICE

*Practice until you can run almost as fast with the ball as you can without it, change direction and still keep control of the ball. As you dribble, keep the ball within touching distance—don't kick the ball and chase it.*

You can use *faking* and *feinting* to fool an opponent about where you are going with a ball.

▶ You are faking when you use your head or body to look or turn in one direction and move the ball in another direction.

◀ You are feinting when you pretend to hesitate or change speed. The idea is to get your opponent moving out of your way.

# Trapping

Receiving and controlling a pass is called trapping. The basic foot trap is used to stop the ball, to change the direction and speed to pass it to a teammate, or to begin moving with it yourself.

▶ Your trapping foot should be raised and at right angles to the foot you are standing on. This forms a corner that helps to confine the ball.

## PARENTS

Always be a **positive example** of dignity, patience, and **good sportsmanship** before, during, and after the game.

▼ Bring the ball of your foot down on the top of the ball. The more of your foot you have on the ball the more control you have.

▼ Always trap downward giving the ball a slight backspin to keep it near to you, but don't pin it to the ground.

You can also use your thigh or chest to knock the ball down to your feet and bring it under control.

▲ Use the lower part of your thigh.

▼ When you use your chest, take it high on the chest to absorb the impact by dropping slightly back and angling the ball to the ground.

Keep your hands slightly behind you—be careful not to touch the ball with your hands.

## PRACTICE

You can practice passing and trapping by yourself by kicking the ball at a wall and then trapping it when it comes back toward you.

The best way to improve your dribbling, trapping, and ball handling skills is to practice with a friend or family member often. These skills are important but come game time strong passing skills are key. It may be tempting to keep the ball as much as possible, but you can help your team out far more by finding open teammates and getting the ball to them.

# Passing

Passing is a fundamental and powerful skill you should practice constantly. The push pass is the most basic kick in soccer.

- ✪ Your non-kicking foot should be next to the ball and facing in the direction you plan to move the ball.

- ✪ Your center of gravity should be over the ball.

- ✪ Bring your kicking leg back a little, turn your knee and foot at right angles to your other foot.

- ✪ Your heel should be down, toes up, and your ankle locked.

- ✪ Swing your foot toward the ball and kick the ball with the inside of your foot on the arch.

*Since the object is to give your teammates an easy ball to handle, use just enough speed to get it to your teammates quickly.*

Don't wait for the ball... move to it.

A longer pass may require you to kick slightly under the ball with the top of your shoe (right), and it may take a bigger follow-through (below).

# Heading

Using your head in soccer doesn't just mean thinking straight! You can use your head to clear the ball from danger and for shooting and passing.

There are just a few basic rules for taking a header.

- Hit the ball with your forehead near your hairline, not the top of your head—that can hurt.

- Keep your eyes open so you know where the ball is coming from and so you can hit it squarely.

- Arch your back and move forward from the waist to meet the ball.

- Clench your teeth and keep your neck firm.

**Open your eyes!**

## PRACTICE

*Start practicing headers with both feet on the ground. Later you can practice jumping to meet the ball.*

**PARENTS**

Show **respect** to the players on **both teams**.

**REMEMBER**

**Go to the ball and control it. Don't just let it hit you on the head!**

Heading **19**

# Juggling

Juggling helps you to develop control of the ball. Practice bouncing the ball as many times as you can without dropping it. Circus jugglers can use their hands, but you can only use your thighs, feet, chest, and head!

Throw the ball a little way into the air, and bring your knee up so the ball bounces off your thigh. While the ball is in the air, lower your leg and then raise it again to meet the ball. See how many times you can do this without stopping.

Try the same thing with your feet. Point your toe, keep your ankle locked, and hit the ball with the part of your foot where your shoelaces are.

Now try using your feet, thighs, and even your head. Hit the ball with your forehead and with your eyes open. Lean your head back and bend your knees a little.

As you improve, juggle the ball with all the different parts of your body except your hands and arms. Try to touch and control the ball with the nearest or most effective body part.

Juggling    **21**

# Shooting and Other Kicks

Shooting is a lot like passing but faster and sometimes farther. The object is to score a goal.

- ✪ Approach the ball from your non-kicking side.

- ✪ Your non-kicking foot should be next to the ball and facing in the direction you plan to move the ball.

- ✪ Your kicking leg knee should be over the ball.

- ✪ Bring your kicking leg back a little with your foot straight on to the ball.

- ✪ Your ankle should be locked, toes down.

- ✪ Keep your head down and your eyes on the ball.

- ✪ Bring your kicking leg down and kick the ball so that your shoelaces touch the ball. The harder and faster you swing your leg, the harder and faster the ball will move. The angle of your foot to the ball will determine the path of the ball. Try slight variations and see what happens.

▲ Swing your leg back hard when you need to get the ball far down the field.

## WHICH DIRECTION?

1. Swerves to the left.
2. Swerves to the right.
3. Straight ahead, keeping low.
4. Straight ahead, rising.

## PRACTICE

You should practice kicking with both feet, not just your stronger leg. Improve your accuracy by imagining a particular spot in the net and then vary your kicks until you hit that spot.

PARENTS

Always **support** your team. Remember, **everyone** makes mistakes. You win **or lose** as a team!

Kick with your laces not your toes. Remember, practice with both feet.

Shooting and Other Kicks    23

In a game, you can never tell when you will get the chance to shoot the ball or from where you will have to shoot it.

Free kicks, like goal kicks and corner kicks, may be taken by any member of the team, so that means everyone should practice the different kinds of kicks and learn what works best in different situations.

bicycle kick

goal kick

corner kick

# Throw-ins

When the ball crosses the touchline, it is put back into play by a throw-in. The player nearest to the ball from the team that did *not* put it over the touchline is given the ball. If that player doesn't do the throw-in correctly, the referee will then give the other team a chance, so practice these regularly. Everyone on the team needs to practice throw-ins.

- ✪ Stand on or behind the touchline at the spot where the ball crossed the line. Stand with both feet on the ground.

- ✪ Hold the ball at the sides with both hands and with your fingers spread out for a good grip.

- ✪ Keep both hands on the ball until you release it.

- ✪ Hold the ball over or behind your head with your elbows bent, lean back a little, and bend your knees slightly.

**TIP!**
If you have a tendency to lift a foot, practice dragging that toe so it doesn't leave the ground.

- ✪ Using both arms, throw the ball forward. Bend forward from the waist as you throw. Keep both hands overhead, not to the side, as you throw.

- ✪ Follow through with your arms and wrists.

- ✪ Keep both feet on the ground during the entire throwing motion.

- ✪ Aim at your teammates' feet so they can receive it easily.

# Shielding

Part of maintaining possession of the ball while you are dribbling is shielding the ball from the defenders.

✪ The best way to shield the ball is to keep the side of your body toward your opponent and between the ball and your opponent. If you completely turn your back to the other player, that player might have an easy shot at the ball from between your legs.

✪ You can keep your arms a little out from your sides for balance, but be careful not to raise them too far or put them too far back—the referee might call a foul.

**TIP!**
Always keep your arms below chest height while shielding or you will be called for a penalty.

## PRACTICE

*A good practice is to work with another player. While you dribble, the other player tries to take the ball from you. Then you do the same while the other player dribbles.*

All the skills in this section up to now have been *offensive* skills—skills you use when your team has possession of the ball. The next three skills are *defensive* skills—skills you need to either keep the other team from scoring or to get the ball so your team can score.

# Marking

When you are assigned a player to mark, your job is to stay with that player.

⊗ Know where the other player is on the field. If he or she doesn't have the ball, your job is to see that he or she can't receive a pass.

⊗ When the other player gets the ball, your job is to try and take it away. This is called *tackling*.

⊗ When you can't take the ball away, you need to make it as difficult as possible to reach your goal.

⊗ Your position is between your opponent and your goal, so you will spend a lot of time running backwards and sideways.

**PRACTICE**

*Practice running in short bursts, stopping quickly, changing direction, and running sideways and backwards.*

**PARENTS**
Always **applaud and cheer** good plays by **both teams**.

**TIP!**
The hips don't lie! No matter how much faking and feinting a player does, you can always tell where a player is going by the direction of the hips.

# Tackling

Unless you've done a good job marking, you may never get a chance to tackle. As with dribbling, you can use your body to fool opponents into moving in the direction you want them to go. The idea is to make it easier for you to get at the ball. You can slow opponents down, make them kick the ball too far ahead, or lose their balance so they kick the ball badly.

You need to keep your eyes open so that when opponents do lose control, you can kick or hook the ball away from them.

There are two basic tackles: the block tackle and the sliding tackle. The block tackle is used to get possession of the ball and keep it. The sliding tackle is used to knock the ball away from your opponent; if you do it well, you jump back up with the ball at your feet. The sliding tackle is much more exciting, but since you nearly always lose your balance and fall, it does mean you are out of play until you get back on your feet. Because getting up takes time, it's good to have a teammate ready to take the ball before you try a sliding tackle in a game.

▼ The block tackle is fastest for taking the ball and moving up the field.

**Block Tackle** With your weight well balanced over your supporting foot, put your other foot as close to the center of the ball as you can. Hook the ball rather than kick it so that you can keep the ball, close to you. Once you have the ball you can dribble or pass it to another player.

**Sliding Tackle** Bend your supporting leg and stretch out the other leg as far as you need to kick the ball away from your opponent.

▶ After a sliding tackle, you must get on your feet before playing the ball.

# Goalkeeping

The goalkeeper (or goalie) is the only player on a team who can legally touch the ball with his or her hands while it is in active play. Although the goalie can kick or knock the ball out of the goal area, the surest way of preventing a goal is for the goalie to catch the ball in both hands. If you are the goalie, you should do the following:

✪ Keep your eyes on the game at all times. Know where the ball is coming from. Be ready to move in any direction at all times.

✪ Move with the play of the ball, keeping your body between the ball and the goal.

✪ Stand in front of the goal in the goal area, but not so far out that the ball can get around you and not on the goal line because the speed of the ball may push you over the line.

✪ Stand facing the field with your knees bent and your feet far enough apart for good balance. Lean forward and keep your hands loose and in front of you so you are ready for the ball.

✪ When you catch the ball, use both hands and spread your fingers wide to grasp as much of the ball as you can. Form a "W" with your hands.

▲ Form hands into a "W" shape

Watch the other players on the field—even the ones without the ball.
A quick pass could catch you off guard.

*As goalie, you are the last defender, but you are also the first
offensive player. You need to get the ball back out to your team
by either throwing it or punting it. Just remember, you can't
leave the goal area with the ball in your hands.*

Talk to your teammates.
Look to see which side is
open. Make sure they are
going where you intend
to punt the ball.

# RULES AND REGULATIONS

occer is played on a flat field. The size of the field and the rules may vary depending on the age of the players and the number of the players, as shown in the chart on page 37. For example, the offside rule is not used in games with fewer than 11 players on each side.

The outside edge of the field is called the **touchline** at the sides and the **goal line** at the ends. Across the center of the field is the **halfway line**. At the center of the field is a circle called the **center circle**. The **center spot** is in the center of that circle. At each end is a **goal**. In front of the goalposts is an area called the **goal area**. The area in front of, and outside of, the goalposts is called the **penalty area**. The **penalty spot** is within the penalty area. The space around the penalty area in a semicircle but outside the penalty area is called the **penalty arc**.

At each corner of the field is the **corner area**.

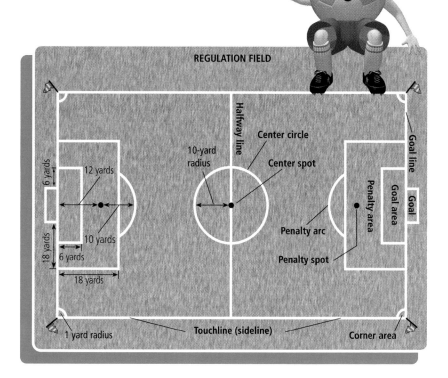

REGULATION FIELD

6 yards
12 yards
10-yard radius
Halfway line
Center circle
Center spot
Penalty area
Goal area
Goal line
Goal
18 yards
10 yards
6 yards
18 yards
Penalty arc
Penalty spot
1 yard radius
Touchline (sideline)
Corner area

# Youth Soccer Most Widely Recommended Field Sizes

| Ages | Field size (I) | Goal size |
|------|----------------|-----------|
| 5 and under | 30 yards long<br>20 yards wide | 1⅓ yards wide<br>6 feet high |
| 6 and 7 | 40 yards long<br>20 yards wide | 2½ yards wide<br>6 feet high |
| 8 to 11 | 80 yards long<br>55 yards wide | 3½ yards wide<br>7 feet high |
| 12 and older | 100–130 yards long<br>50–100 yards wide | 8 yards wide<br>8 feet high |

# Ball Sizes, Team Sizes, and Length of Games

| Ages | Ball Size (II) | Number of Players | Length of Game (VII) |
|------|----------------|-------------------|----------------------|
| 5 and under | Size 3<br>23–24" circ.<br>10–12 ounces | 3 v. 3 | 30 minutes<br>2 15-minute halves |
| 6 and 7 | Size 3<br>23–24" circ.<br>10–12 ounces | 4 v. 4 | 40 minutes<br>2 20-minute halves |
| 8 to 10 | Size 4<br>25–26" circ.<br>12–14 ounces | 6 v. 6 | 50 minutes<br>2 25-minute halves |
| 11 to 12 | Size 4<br>25–26" circ.<br>12–14 ounces | 11 v. 11 | 50 minutes<br>2 25-minute halves |
| 13 to 15 | Size 5<br>27–28" circ.<br>14–16 ounces | 11 v. 11 | 50 minutes<br>2 25-minute halves |
| 16 and older | Size 5<br>27–28" circ. | 11 v. 11 | 90 minutes<br>2 45-minute halves |

Note Roman numerals in parentheses refer to rule numbers of the Official Rules of Soccer of the U.S. Soccer Federation. Read these rules for more in-depth explanations. Keep in mind that rules may vary by town and league.

# Player Positions (III)

All players can play both offensive and defensive positions.

**Forwards** Forwards are *offensive* players—they play closest to the opposing team's goal. It is their job to get the ball into the net. The players who play near the touchlines are called **wings;** the players in the middle of the field are called **strikers.** Forwards need to learn to dribble, pass, and shoot.

**Halfbacks** Halfbacks (midfielders) are all-purpose players. Their job is to prevent the ball from getting down the field to their team's defenders and move the ball up the field to their team's forwards. They can take shots and try to take the ball from the other team's players. Midfielders do most of the throw-ins.

**Fullbacks** Fullbacks (defenders) play near their own team's goal. Their job is to prevent the other team from shooting and to get the ball away from the goal. They can receive the ball from the goalkeeper. They move the ball back toward the center of the field so the midfielders can begin the offensive play. A defensive player with no specific opponent to mark, therefore at liberty to gain possession of the ball or to move on any unmarked player who moves into a dangerous position, is called a sweeper.

**PARENTS**

Let the **coaches** do the coaching.

**Goalkeeper** The keeper, or goalie, plays in front of the goal and tries to stop the ball from getting into the net. The goalie is the only player allowed to use his or her hands in a game (but only within the goal area). Goalies are responsible for directing the defensive play by telling the defenders who to mark. They also defend against penalty kicks. Goalies need to be able to punt and throw the ball long distances.

# Player Equipment (IV)

The standard uniform is a colored, or patterned, team shirt and shorts, socks worn over shinpads, and soccer cleats. The keeper may also wear gloves and a padded jersey and shorts, or pants, in addition to elbow and knee pads.

No watches or jewelry of any sort is allowed. Players should not wear anything that might hurt themselves or others during play.

# REFEREES (V)

> **Listen to the referee. The ref's decision is final.**

The referee has many jobs.
The referee:

- Starts the game and acts as timekeeper
- Sees that all the rules are followed
- Decides when the ball is out of bounds and when corner kicks, goal kicks, and throw-ins are allowed
- Decides when a player should be penalized for being in an offside position (see p. 45)
- Decides on penalties for misconduct

*The referee can even stop the game if he or she feels that the players or fans are getting out of control.*

## REFEREE SIGNALS

▲ **Advantage/Play on**
When the referee spots a foul, but sees that stopping play would help the team that committed the foul, the referee indicates to play on and points in the direction the advancing team is going.

▲ **Penalty Kick**
If a defending team commits a foul in its goal area, the offense is awarded a penalty kick, and the referee points to the penalty mark.

**◀ Corner Kick**
If the defense has kicked a ball over the goal line and outside the goalposts, the referee points to the corner mark where the offense will take a corner kick.

**▲ Goal Kick**
When the offense has kicked a ball over the goal line and outside of the goalposts, the referee points to the goalie box where the defense will take a goal kick.

**◀ Direct Free Kick**
The referee indicates the direction and approximate position of the direct free kick.

**▶ Caution or expulsion**
When a player has committed a dangerous foul or has used unsportsman-like behavior, a card is raised to indicate caution or expulsion. The player's name is also recorded.

**▲ Indirect Free Kick**
The referee keeps this position until an indirect free kick has been taken and the ball is touched by the other team or has gone out of bounds.

## LINESMEN SIGNALS

**▲ Substitution**
The assistant referee holds the flag up with both hands to signal the referee a substitution.

**▲ Throw-in**
The assistant referee indicates the direction in which the ball should be returned to play. If the offense is headed that direction, it throws in the ball. If the defense is headed that direction, it throws in the ball.

**▲ Goal Kick**
The assistant referee points to the goalie box to indicate a goal kick.

**▲ Corner Kick**
The assistant referee closest to a corner kick will indicate the position of that kick. The assistant might wait a moment to look at the referee in case the referee has already decided and indicated.

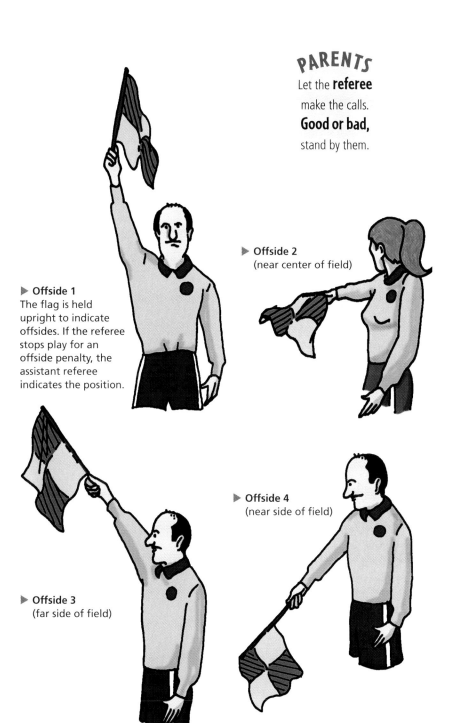

**PARENTS**
Let the **referee** make the calls. **Good or bad,** stand by them.

▶ **Offside 2**
(near center of field)

▶ **Offside 1**
The flag is held upright to indicate offsides. If the referee stops play for an offside penalty, the assistant referee indicates the position.

▶ **Offside 4**
(near side of field)

▶ **Offside 3**
(far side of field)

# Duration of the Game (VII)

A regulation 11 v. 11 game has two 45-minute halves. Youth soccer games can be shorter (see chart on page 37). Time can be extended at the end of a normal period for a penalty kick. Allowances can be made for substitutions and other delays. The halftime interval is usually 15 minutes, but can be changed with the consent of the referee. The winner of a tied game can be determined by penalty kicks in some situations.

# Start of Play (VIII)

Before the game starts, the referee meets with the two team captains for the coin toss. The winner chooses which goal to attack for the first half of the game and the loser kicks off.

At the referee's signal to start the game, the chosen player makes a place-kick into the other team's end of the field (or passes the ball forward to a teammate). A kickoff is also a way to restart a game after a goal or at the start of an overtime period.

After halftime, play is restarted in the same way by a player of the other team. Teams change ends and attack the other goal.

The kicker cannot touch the ball again until it has been touched by another player. If the player does touch the ball, the other team will get an indirect free kick from the place where the kicker touched the ball.

A goal can be scored from the kickoff.

After any other suspensions in play, the referee will drop the ball at the place where the play was stopped unless it has crossed the touchline or goal line. The ball is not in play until it has touched the ground.

# The Ball In and Out of Play (IX)

The ball is out of play when it is completely across the touchline or goal line, or when the referee has stopped the game.

The ball is in play if it rebounds from a goalpost, crossbar, or corner flag into the field of play, if it rebounds off the referee if he or she is in the field of play, or until a decision is made about a broken rule.

# Scoring (X)

A goal is scored only when the whole ball has passed over the goal line between the goalposts, provided it has not been thrown or carried by a player of the attacking side. A goal is worth one point. The team with the most goals wins.

# Offside (XI)

An offensive player is in an offside position when he or she is between the goal and the last defender (other than the goalie) at the moment the ball is played to him or her by a teammate.

A player will only be penalized for being in an offside position if he or she is interfering with play, an opponent, or is seeking to gain an advantage at the moment the ball touches or is played by a teammate.

A player will not be penalized for being in an offside position when receiving the ball directly from a goal kick, corner kick, or throw-in.

The penalty for being offside is an indirect free kick for the opposing team.

# Fouls and Misconduct (XII)

Kicking or attempting to kick, tripping, jumping at, charging at, hitting, spitting at, holding, or pushing an opponent will be penalized by a direct free kick from the spot where the offense occurred. Carrying, striking, or propelling the ball with a hand or arm will also be penalized by a direct free kick from the spot where the foul occurred.

If a player of the defending team commits any of these offenses within the penalty area, he or she will be penalized by a penalty kick.

An indirect free kick results from: playing in a manner considered dangerous, charging with the shoulder when the ball is not within playing distance, impeding the progress of an opponent when not attempting to play the ball, charging the goalkeeper except when he or she has the ball or is outside the goal area, or violating the offside rule. A goalkeeper can be penalized for touching the ball with hands or arms outside the penalty area, wasting time, or delaying the game to give an unfair advantage to the goalkeeper's own team.

# Cautions and Ejections

A player will be cautioned and shown a yellow card by the referee if he or she deliberately and continually commits violations of the rules.

A player will be shown a red card and ejected by the referee if he or she has been guilty of violent conduct, serious foul play, foul or abusive language, or an offense that already yielded one caution.

The guilty player cannot return to the game or be replaced by a substitute.

# Free Kicks (XIII)

A goal can be scored with a direct free kick. A goal cannot be scored with an indirect free kick unless it has been played or touched by a player from either team before passing through the goal area.

When a player is taking a free kick inside his or her own penalty area, opposing team players must be at least 10 yards from the ball and must remain outside the penalty area until the ball has been kicked out of the penalty area.

When a player takes a free kick outside the penalty area, all of the opposing players must be at least 10 yards from the ball unless they are on their own goal line between the goalposts.

The kicker cannot play the ball a second time until it has been touched by another player. If he or she does, a free kick will be given to the opposing team.

Free kicks awarded to the defending team may be taken from within the goal area.

Indirect free kicks given to the attacking team within the opposing team's goal area must be taken from the goal area line parallel to the goal line and nearest the point where the offense was committed.

This is going to sting!

# Penalty Kick (XIV)

A penalty kick is taken from the penalty mark. All players except for the player taking the kick and the opposing team's goalkeeper must be outside the penalty area.

The goalkeeper must stand without moving his or her feet on the goal line between the goalposts until the ball is kicked. The kicker cannot touch the ball again until it has been played by another player.

A goal may be scored from a penalty kick.

# Throw-ins (XV)

When the ball completely crosses the touchline it is thrown back into play by a member of the team opposing that of the player who last touched it. The player throwing in cannot then touch the ball again until it has been played by another player.

A player throwing in must stand on or behind the touchline and keep both feet on the ground while taking the throw. The ball is thrown with both hands from over the head. A goal cannot be scored from a throw-in.

Remember, if you pick up your back toe or throw with only one hand, the other team gets the ball.

# Goal Kick (XVI)

When the ball has been kicked over the goal line outside the goalposts by the opposing team, it can be kicked back into play beyond the penalty area by any player of the defending team. If the ball is not kicked beyond the penalty area, the goal kick may be taken again.

The goalkeeper cannot receive the ball from a goal kick.

The player taking the goal kick cannot touch the ball again until it has been played by another player. If he or she does, an indirect free kick will be given to the opposing team.

# Corner Kick (XVII)

When the ball has been kicked over the goal line outside the goalposts by the defending team, any player from the opposing team can take a corner kick. Defending players must be 10 yards away from the ball. The ball is placed in the corner of the field nearest to the point where the ball crossed the goal line.

A goal may be scored from a corner kick.

The player taking the corner kick cannot touch the ball again until it has been played by another player. If he or she does, an indirect free kick will be given to the opposing team.

# DICTIONARY OF COMMON SOCCER TERMS

**Advantage Law** The rule that allows play to continue after a foul if stopping the action would prove advantageous to the team that made it.

**Angle, Narrowing the** When defenders, including the goalkeeper, move closer to the ball to reduce the angle for passing or shooting.

**Association Football** The international name for soccer.

**AYSO** American Youth Soccer Organization.

**Ball** Soccer balls come in three basic sizes, see page 37. Balls should always be properly inflated; improperly inflated balls could lead to injury. Practice with a ball is critical. If at all possible, your child should own one.

**Ball-watching** When players are unaware of the movements of the players they are assigned to mark because they are so intent on watching the ball.

**Ball carrier** The player with the ball.

**Basket-hanging** A term borrowed from basketball and referring to a player who stays near the opposition net even when the ball is far away.

**Bicycle kick** A backward, overhead kick.

**Booking** When the referee writes down the name of a player as a warning that any further misconduct will result in an ejection.

**Break-away** When a player breaks away from a defender and charges the goalie.

**Cap** When a player plays for the National Team in an official international competition like the World Cup or World Cup qualifying matches.

**Caution** When a player gets a yellow card.

**Center circle** The circle in the middle of the field where play begins at the start of each half and after each goal. See page 36. Defenders may not enter the circle until the ball rolls one full turn.

**Center forward** Another name for a striker.

**Center line** The line which divides the field in half. See page 36.

**Center the ball** To pass the ball to the middle of the field, usually to the penalty area, from the sideline.

**Changing the field** Moving the ball across the field from the crowded side to the more open side, usually with a single long pass.

**Charging** When a player leans into an opponent with his or her shoulder. It is legal as long as the player does not lean too far or ram the opponent off balance.

**Clear** A hard defensive, frequently unaimed, kick to clear the ball from in front of the goal.

**Cleats** Special footwear for soccer. The ball control surfaces should be smooth. Cleats are absolutely necessary for balance and changing direction quickly. Cleats cannot be pointy and must be at least ½ inch wide and no more than ¾ inch deep.

**Coin toss** At the start of each game a coin is tossed. The winning side gets to choose which side of the field to play for the first half and the losing team kicks off.

**Corner kick** When a ball has been kicked over the goal line by a defender, the opposition is awarded a free kick. This kick is taken from the corner area nearest to where the ball crossed the line.

**Cross, Diagonal** A ball played forward from right to left or left to right. Usually played in the offensive third of the field.

**Cross, Far Post** A pass kicked to the far side of the goal.

**Cross, Near Post** A pass kicked to the near side of the goal.

**Cross** Same as a center.

**Crossbar** The top horizontal section of the goalposts.

**Dangerous play** An action that puts a player at risk of injury. It is punished by an indirect free kick.

**Dead ball** A ball put into play from a free kick. Also a ball not in motion when the player kicks it.

**Defender** A player playing in his or her end of the field engaged in preventing the opposition from scoring.

**Direct free kick** A kick awarded for a deliberate foul. These fouls include: kicking, jumping, striking, tripping, holding, pushing another player, charging into another player, and touching the ball with the hand or arm. A goal may be scored from a direct free kick. See also indirect free kick.

**Dribbling** Moving the ball along the ground with the feet.

**Driving** Pushing the ball into spaces and moving after it.

**Drop ball** A referee can put a ball back into play by dropping it between a player from each team. The ball must hit the ground before it can be played. May be used when a referee does not know who touched the ball last.

**Dummy** A feint where a receiver pretends to touch or kick the ball but allows it to run past or between his or her legs to another teammate running behind.

**Faking** Moving the head or body or looking in one direction while actually planning to move in another to fool the opponent.

**Far post** The goalpost that is farthest from the ball. A shooter should try to shoot between the far post and the goalie. It allows more time for the ball to curve into the goal, or for another chance if the shot misses.

**Feinting** Pretending to hesitate or change speed to fool an opponent into moving in another direction.

**Fédération Internationale de Football Association (FIFA)** The international governing body of football (soccer), headquartered in Zurich, Switzerland, and the sponsors of the World Cup. FIFA sets rules and settles disputes. The USSF and CSA are members of FIFA.

**Finish** To execute a shot or a center pass while in a dead run.

**First-timing** To kick the ball without trapping it first.

**Flags** The four corners of the field are marked by flags.

**Flight** The path of the ball through the air.

**Football** Worldwide term for soccer.

**Forward** A player who plays close to the opposition goal. There are wing forwards, center forwards, inside forwards, and strikers.

**Free kick** Free kicks include penalty kicks, goal kicks, corner kicks, and direct and indirect free kicks. They are kicks taken to restart play after a foul, a score, or when the ball goes over the goal line.

**Fullback** A defender positioned close to the sideline. There are wing fullbacks, center fullbacks, sweepers, and stoppers.

**Goal kick** A free kick taken by the defending team when the ball has been kicked over the goal line, but not into the goal, by the attacking team. It must be outside the penalty area before any player can play the ball.

**Goal line** The end boundary line running parallel to the goalposts.

**Goalkeeper** (goalie, keeper) The player who remains in the goal area and defends the goal from the attacking team. He or she is the only player allowed to use hands.

**Half volley** Kicking the ball at the moment the ball bounces.

**Halfback** Players who play in the middle of the field. There are wing or side halfbacks, and center halfbacks.

**Hand ball** When a player touches the ball with a hand and/or arm. A direct free kick is given to the opposing team.

**Hat trick** When a player scores three or more goals in one game. Also can be used when a team wins three or more games in a row.

**Heading** Using the head to play the ball.

**Indirect free kick** A free kick given for unintentional fouls, obstruction, or dangerous play. On an indirect free kick, the ball must be touched by another player before a goal can be scored.

**Injury time** When a game is stopped because of injuries, the scoring of a goal, or time-wasting, time is added to the end of the game.

**Instep kick** A kick taken with the upper surface of the foot. It is a particularly powerful and accurate kick.

**Juggling** An exercise used to improve ball control in which a player uses any part of his or her body, except for the hands and arms, to stop the ball from touching the ground.

**Keepaway** Keeping possession while preventing an opponent from getting the ball.

**Kickoff** A kick taken at the start of each half, when a goal has been scored, or at the start of an overtime period. Two players stand within the center circle with the ball. All other players must stand outside the center circle. The ball is in play when it is kicked and moved forward.

**Linesmen** Officials who aid the referee. Their job is to watch the sidelines and signal to the referee when the ball goes out of bounds or when they see an offside or other infractions.

**Manager** Coach.

**Marking** Defensive play in which each player is assigned an attacking player to mark or guard. The players' job is to prevent the opposing player from receiving the ball.

**Midfielder** Players who play in the middle of the field. There are wing or side midfielders and center midfielders.

**Midfield** The middle third of the field.

**MLS** Major League Soccer.

**National Team** Players, usually professionals, who play for their country in international competitions, such as the World Cup.

**National Youth Team** Players under 19 who play for their country in international competitions, such as the FIFA Youth Championship.

**NCAA: National Collegiate Athletic Association** The major body of college soccer in the U.S.

**Near post** The goalpost closest to an attacker with the ball.

**Obstruction** When a player deliberately blocks an opponent from playing the ball. An indirect free kick is awarded against the obstructing player.

**Off-the-ball movement** A move by attacking players, not in possession of the ball, to create open space for a teammate.

**Offside** An attacking player is considered offside when he or she is between the goal and the ball at the time the ball is played by the attacking team if there are not at least two defending players (including the keeper) between the player and the goal. An offensive player is not offside when he or she is receiving a goal kick, corner kick, throw-in, or drop ball. A player may move up past the ball once it is in motion. The rule is designed to prevent players from bunching up around the goal to wait for a pass. An indirect free kick is awarded against a player who is offside.

**Pass, Chip** Kicking the ball into the air with a backspin by stabbing at the bottom of it.

**Pass, Flick** Kicking the ball with the outside of the foot.

**Pass, Push** Kicking the ball with the inside of the foot. One of the most used passes in soccer.

**Pass, Volley** Making contact with the ball before it hits the ground as in volleyball.

**Pass, Wall** Where the receiver returns the ball to the passer at an angle similar to that at which the player received it.

**Penalties** Free kicks awarded by the referee for fouls and misconduct.

**Penalty arc** Semicircle 10 yards in radius extending from the penalty spot.

**Penalty area** Area in front of the goal where the goalie may use hands to catch or block the ball. This area is 44 yards wide and 18 yards deep on a regulation soccer field.

**Penalty kick** A direct free kick awarded when a player commits a major foul within his or her own penalty area. It is taken from the penalty spot. On a full-size field the penalty spot is 12 yards in front of the goal. Only the goalie is permitted inside the goal area during a free kick. All other players must stand outside the penalty area. The goalie must have both feet on the goal line until the ball is kicked.

**Penetrating pass** A pass that goes past one or more defensive players before reaching the receiver.

**Penetration** Moving deeply into the opposition's end of the field. Wings and strikers should always try to penetrate as far as the offside rule allows.

**Professional foul** A foul committed by a defensive player against the ball carrier just outside of the penalty area.

**Red card** The signal for ejection. It is usually issued after a yellow card warning has already been given.

**Redirecting** Altering the angle and flight of the ball.

**Referee** The final authority who runs the game on the field, keeps the time, and controls play.

**Run-off-the-ball** To get into position to help the team when not in possession of the ball, or to try and create an open space.

**Save** When the keeper prevents a goal by catching or deflecting the ball.

**Scissors kick** See bicycle kick.

**Screening** Staying between the defender and the ball to prevent the defender from getting a kick at it.

**Shielding** Using the body to keep the defender from touching the ball without fouling.

**Shin guards** Padding worn on the legs under socks to protect the shins from damage.

**Sideline** Border of the playing field that runs perpendicular to the goal line.

**Side-foot kick** A kick taken with the side of the foot.

**Sliding tackle** A defensive move where the player slides at the ball in an attempt to knock the ball away from the attacker and/or gain control.

**Small-sided game** A game played by fewer than 11 players to a side, usually played on a smaller-than-regulation field.

**Soccer** The American name for Association Football.

**Stopper** The defensive player used to block and repel the attack in the center of the field. The player usually marks the opposition's striker.

**Striker** The offensive player whose main task is to play forward, receive passes, and attempt to score goals.

**Strong side** Area of the field to the side of the goal that is closer to the ball.

**Sudden death** Tie-breaking procedure where the play continues until a team has scored.

**Supporting** See off-the-ball movement.

**Sweeper** A defensive player with no specific opponent to mark. Therefore, he or she is at liberty to gain possession of the ball or to move on any unmarked player who moves into a dangerous position.

**Tackle** To attempt to gain legal possession of the ball by blocking the ball with the feet and legs.

**Through pass** A pass played past the defense to an open space where an attacker can run for it.

**Throw-in** When a ball is knocked out of bounds along the sidelines, a throw-in is awarded to the opposing team. The player doing the throw-in stands with both feet behind the touchline and throws the ball with both hands in an overhead motion. A goal cannot be scored directly from a throw-in.

**Total soccer** Soccer play where all of a team's players attack when their side has the ball and all defend when without it.

**Touch** To make contact with the ball. One-touch is to receive and then pass in the same single contact. Two-touch is to trap it and then pass it with the next touch.

**Touchline** Sideline.

**Trapping** To bring the ball under control. Any part of the body can be used except the hands or arms.

**USSF** United States Soccer Federation, the governing body of organized soccer in this country, an affiliate of FIFA.

**USYSA** United States Youth Soccer Association. The branch of the USSF that oversees soccer for players ages 19 and under.

**Volley** Kicking a ball in midair.

**Weak side** The area of the field to the side of the goal farther from the ball.

**Winger** The forward who plays on the outside of the field. The player's responsibility is to set up teammates for scoring opportunities.

**Winghalf** The midfielder who plays on the outside of the field.

**World Cup** The international tournament played every four years. Teams of almost 150 countries compete in regional competitions until 22 finalists join the previous cup's winner and the host country's national team for the final tournament. Officially the Jules Rimet Trophy, named after the Frenchman who founded the tournament.

**Yellow card** A card held up to signal a warning to a player that any further misconduct will result in that player being ejected from the game.

# GAMES

BALL
DRIBBLE
FAKE
FOOT
GAME

GOAL
KICK
KEEPER
NET
PASS

PENALTY
PLAY
RED
SOCCER
STRIKER

SWEEPER
TEAM
THROW
TRAP
WIN

```
F  O  O  T  Z  O  L  D  Q  I  P  K
L  F  F  E  A  M  Q  P  T  X  Z  E
L  F  W  A  D  D  R  I  B  B  L  E
R  Y  U  M  S  V  K  L  Z  X  C  P
P  A  S  S  O  W  A  C  N  J  L  E
E  R  Y  U  P  D  E  G  A  S  U  R
N  C  D  G  F  A  K  E  Z  W  Q  M
A  R  S  B  N  U  Y  I  P  P  W  T
L  I  N  C  E  M  Q  S  T  E  Y  L
T  R  A  P  C  T  D  L  C  F  R  L
Y  E  T  L  K  R  W  X  T  N  Q  S
U  D  G  A  M  E  E  K  L  E  Z  N
H  J  D  Y  B  M  N  Q  R  J  N  B
M  B  S  O  C  C  E  R  F  E  S  A
S  E  T  C  B  N  T  U  W  S  Q  L
D  F  R  M  R  W  D  Y  G  O  A  L
Z  W  I  N  T  X  L  C  V  B  L  V
I  X  K  I  C  K  O  E  Z  E  M  E
N  V  E  R  S  W  S  L  O  W  W  U
T  H  R  O  W  T  E  E  Q  M  E  K
```

**WORD FIND**

# CROSSWORD

## ACROSS

1 Person with final decision-making power

4 Forward most responsible for scoring goals

9 To look one way and go another way

10 A ball going into the net scores a _ _ _ _.

11 Type of leg guard

12 Soccer is a _ _ _ _ _.

13 Card held in the air by referee as an official warning that further misconduct will result in ejection

14 Boys and _ _ _ _ _ play soccer.

16 Kick taken at start of each half

18 When goalkeepers prevent a score, they make a _ _ _ _.

21 Card held in the air by the referee to reject a player from the game

22 You use your feet in _ _ _ _ _ _.

23 To kick the ball at the net.

## DOWN

2 Attacking player who is closest to the other team's goal

3 Soccer is played with a _ _ _ _.

5 To resume play after a stop in the action

6 Kicking the ball in midair

7 Pass made with the inside of the foot

8 Soccer is _ _ _.

10 To resume play when the attacking team last touched the ball before crossing goal line

12 Extra defender with no special opponent

15 Only player who can touch the ball with hands.

17 Type of shoes worn in soccer

19 Keep your _ _ _ _ out a little for balance when doing a throw-in.

20 Initials for Major League Soccer

**ACROSS**

1 REFEREE
4 STRIKER
9 FAKE
10 GOAL
11 SHINPAD
12 SPORT
13 YELLOW CARD
14 GIRLS
16 KICKOFF
18 SAVE
21 RED CARD
22 SOCCER
23 SHOOT

**DOWN**

2 FORWARD
3 BALL
5 RESTART
6 VOLLEY
7 PUSHPASS
8 FUN
10 GOALKICK
12 SWEEPER
15 GOALIE
17 CLEATS
19 ARMS
20 MLS

## Answers to Word Find on page 57

```
F  O  O  T  Z  O  L  D  Q  I  P  K
L  F  F  E  A  M  Q  P  T  X  Z  E
L  F  W  A  D  D  R  I  B  B  L  E
R  Y  U  M  S  V  K  L  Z  X  C  P
P  A  S  S  O  W  A  C  N  J  L  E
E  R  Y  U  P  D  E  G  A  S  U  R
N  C  D  G  F  A  K  E  Z  W  Q  M
A  R  S  B  N  U  Y  I  P  P  W  T
L  I  N  C  E  M  Q  S  T  E  Y  L
T  R  A  P  C  T  D  L  C  F  R  L
Y  E  T  L  K  R  W  X  T  N  Q  S
U  D  G  A  M  E  E  K  L  E  Z  N
H  J  D  Y  B  M  N  Q  R  J  N  B
M  B  S  O  C  C  E  R  F  E  S  A
S  E  T  C  B  N  T  U  W  S  Q  L
D  F  R  M  R  W  D  Y  G  O  A  L
Z  W  I  N  T  X  L  C  V  B  I  V
I  X  K  I  C  K  O  E  Z  E  M  E
N  V  E  R  S  W  S  L  O  W  W  U
T  H  R  O  W  T  E  E  Q  M  E  K
```